DID YOU
HEAR THE ONE ABOUT...

SOUPY SALES
DID YOU
HEAR THE ONE ABOUT...

THE GREATEST JOKES EVER TOLD

COLLIER BOOKS

MACMILLAN PUBLISHING COMPANY

New York

COLLIER MACMILLAN PUBLISHERS

London

Macmillan Publishing Company
866 Third Avenue, New York, N.Y. 10022
Collier Macmillan Canada, Inc.

Library of Congress Cataloging-in-Publication Data
Sales, Soupy.
Soupy Sales' did you hear the one about—.
1. American wit and humor. I. Title.
PN6162.S247 1987   818'.5402   86-26832
ISBN 0-02-040590-1

10 9 8 7 6 5 4 3 2 1

Printed in the United States of America

To Isaac Lerner of Huntington, West Virginia, who said to me in 1946, "Listen, give up all this foolish show-business business. You'll come and work for me in the pawnshop."

And to my mother, Sadie, who said, "Listen to him!"

ACKNOWLEDGMENTS

With deep appreciation to WNBC, WXYZ-TV in Detroit, John Pival, and to my family, my friends, and—above all—my fans.

INTRODUCTION

Isn't it a great feeling to laugh at a joke you've never heard before? And isn't it a great feeling to tell a story and "break up" your friends?

Thus, the greatest stories I've ever heard and told. The clean ones, that is.

I've always found that the answer to good story-telling is to embellish, exaggerate, and tell them in your own style.

This book is not to analyse, teach, instruct, or to educate you. I just hope you enjoy it as much as I have putting it together. They're my favorites and I hope once you read them they'll be your favorites, too.

Soupy Sales

1986

DID YOU
HEAR THE ONE ABOUT...

A stockbroker dies and goes to heaven. As he gets to the pearly gates, St. Peter says to him, "Who are you?" And the guy says, "I'm a Wall Street broker."

So St. Peter says, "What do you want?"

And the stockbroker says, "I want to get in."

And St. Peter says, "What have you done that you think should entitle you to admission?"

So the stockbroker says, "Well, for one thing, I saw a bum on Broadway the other day and I gave him a nickel."

And St. Peter says to Gabriel, "Is that in the records?"

And Gabriel says, "Yes."

"What else have you done?" St. Peter asks the broker.

So the broker says, "Well, the other night I was crossing the Brooklyn Bridge and I ran into a half-frozen newsboy and I gave him a nickel."

And St. Peter says to Gabriel, "Is that in the records?"

And Gabriel says, "Yes, St. Peter."

And St. Peter says to the broker, "What else have you done?"

And the guy says, "That's all I can think of."

And St. Peter says, "What do you think we ought to do with this guy, Gabriel?"

And Gabriel says, "Give him back his dime and tell him to go to hell!"

The firing squad in a South American country is taking a prisoner to a wall where they're gonna shoot him.

It's a dismal, rainy day and they're walking in the mud and getting soaked.

So the condemned prisoner in his torn up clothes, wearing no shoes, looks up and says, "What a terrible day to die."

And one of the guards says, "What are you kicking about? *We* have to walk all the way back in the rain!"

Two guys out fishing in a boat. One guy is catching all the fish. He's reeling them in as fast as he baits his hook. The other guy is going crazy because he's catching nothing. So he says to the guy, "I've been fishing longer than you. I've always caught a lot of fish. I've got better equipment. I have a better rod. I throw my line better. And you're getting all the fish. How do you do it?"

The other guy says, "I play hunches!" And the guy says, "What kind of hunches?" And his friend says, "When I get up in the morning, if my wife is lying on her left side, I fish on the left side of the boat. If she's lying on her right side, I always fish on the right side."

And the other guy says, "Suppose she's lying on her back?"

And his buddy says, "Then I don't go fishing!"

There was this actor who needed an expensive operation, so he goes to the best doctor in town and the doctor does the operation and it's a success!

And the doctor's in his room and gives him a bill for two thousand dollars. The actor says, "I can't afford that." So the doctor says, "Hey, I understand, I'm a big fan of yours, give me a thousand and you'll send me an eight-by-ten glossy, you'll sign 'To My Pal Bernie,' and that'll be fine."

And the actor tells him, "I can't afford that, either." They argue back and forth, the doctor agrees to take $250 for his fee and the doctor says to him, "For that price, you might as well have it for nothing!" And the actor says, "Thanks, Doc, I was hoping you'd say that." And the doctor says to him, "If you knew you couldn't afford my fee, why in the hell did you come to me, the most expensive doctor in town?"

And the actor says, "Listen, where my health is concerned, money is no object!"

A man walks into a psychiatrist's office and says to the doctor, "I've lost all desire to go on. Life is just too fast, too hectic."

And the psychiatrist says, "Yes, I understand. We all have problems. You'll need several years of treatments at fifty dollars an hour."

And for a few moments there's complete silence and the guy says to the psychiatrist, "Well, that solves your problem, Doctor. Now what about mine?"

There are two guys, Smith and Jones, who save up their money and go on a safari to Africa. So after dinner around the campfire one night, Smith bets Jones that he'll be the first one to shoot a lion.

They argue back and forth and finally Smith bets Jones a hundred dollars that he'll be the first. And Smith says, "I'll do it right now." So he loads up his rifle and stalks out of the tent and heads for the jungle.

An hour later a lion pokes his head inside the tent and says, "You know a guy named Smith?"

And Jones, trembling, says, "Yes!"

And the lion says, "Well, he owes you a hundred dollars!"

Everyone at the plant has joined the pension plan except a guy named Seymour. Since the deal depends on 100 percent employee participation, unless Seymour signs, it's a no-go.

Now all his fellows workers plead, cajole, and pressure him to sign, but to no avail. But Seymour is convinced the plan will never pay off and he stands by his convictions.

Finally, the shop steward comes to him and says, "Seymour, if you don't sign, not only will you never work in this industry again, but I personally will break every bone in your body." So Seymour reaches for his pen and signs.

So the shop steward says to him, "Now, can you tell me why it took you so long to come around?" And Seymour says, "You're the first one who's explained it!"

A stockbroker is suffering from a recurring ringing in his ears and he goes to a doctor who recommends that he should have his tonsils removed, but the operation doesn't help. He goes to a second doctor who advises him to have his teeth pulled. This too fails and the ringing continues.

The guy goes to a third specialist who tells him, "I'm sorry to tell you this but you're suffering from a rare disease and at best, you have six months to live."

Since the guy has no relatives to whom to leave his money, he decides to spend every cent he has. He books passage for a trip around the world. Goes to the best tailor and orders twenty handmade suits and goes to a shirtmaker to have his shirts made to order.

So the shirtmaker says, "Let's get your measurements. Thirty-four sleeve, sixteen collar." And the broker says, "No, that's fifteen." The shirtmaker says, "Collar, sixteen. Look at the tape measure." The broker says, "It can't be, I've always worn a fifteen collar and that's what I want."

And the shirtmaker says, "All right, but you'll get a ringing in your ears!"

Acoustic   Something you play pool with—*acoustic.*

Apple Turnover   A command a fruit peddler uses when training an apple.

Bacteria   The back door of a cafeteria.

Bald Eagle   Large bird too vain to buy a hairpiece.

This machine operator comes home from the factory and tells his wife: "Martha, I've got some good news and I've got some bad news. First, the good news: I got twenty-five thousand dollars severance pay."

His wife says, "Twenty-five thousand dollars in severance pay? That's great! Now, what's the bad news?"

And the guy says, "Wait'll you hear what was severed!"

A woman is showing a contractor through the second floor of her new house, advising him what colors to paint the rooms. So she says, "I'd like the bedroom done in blue," and the contractor walks over to the window and shouts, "Green side up! Green side up!"

And the woman continues talking and says, "I want the bathroom in white," and again the contractor yells out the window, "Green side up! Green side up!"

And the woman continues and says to the contractor, "The halls should be done in gray," and again the contractor shouts out the window, "Green side up! Green side up!"

All of a sudden the woman says to him angrily, "Every time I give you a color, you shout 'Green side up!' " and the contractor says, "I'm sorry, ma'am, but I've got three college graduates down there putting in the lawn!"

A bum runs into a friend of his on the road and says, "Man, you ought to be ashamed of yourself, wearing an old, ragged, torn pair of pants like that." And his friend says, "How'm I going to get a pair of new trousers? They don't grow on trees."

So the bum says, "You just go up to the first house that looks like the folks might have an extra pair of trousers and ask for an old pair."

So the ragged bum says okay, and as he walks down the street, he sees a doctor's sign on a house. He walks up to the door and knocks. A lady answers the door and the bum asks her if the doctor is in. The woman says, "Yes," and the bum says, "Will you be kind enough to ask the doctor if he has an old pair of pants he could let me have." And the woman says she couldn't do that. And the bum says, "I don't mind if they're old." And the woman says, "That isn't the problem. I'm the doctor!"

A beautiful blonde in a convertible pulls up to a gas station. And all of a sudden four attendants swarm all over the car. One of them is giving her gas, one is wiping her windshield, one is checking her tires, and one is checking the oil. But a fifth attendant just looks on with a smile.

So one of the attendants stops and asks him, "Aren't you coming over to check something?" And the guy says, "I don't have to. I'm her husband!"

An old man, who's a pretty good drinker and a smart and learned man, is brought up before a country judge.

The judge says, "You're charged with being drunk and disorderly. Have you anything to say why sentence should not be pronounced?"

And the old drunk gets up and looks up at the judge and says, "Man's inhumanity to man makes countless thousands mourn." And he continues, his arms fluttering to the sky, "I'm not so debased as Poe, so ungrateful as Keats, so intemperate as Burns, so timid as Tennyson, so vulgar as Shakespeare, so—"

And the judge says, "Shut up! That'll be ninety days," and he says to the bailiff, "Take down the list of names and round them up, they're as bad as he is!"

There's this woman who plays cards one night a month with a group of her friends. And every time she always wakes up her husband because it's about midnight when she gets in. So one night she decides she won't disturb him. So she gets home after midnight and she undresses in the living room, and with her handbag over her arm, she tiptoes nude into the bedroom—only to find her husband sitting up in bed reading.

He looks up from the paper at her and says, "Good Lord, did you lose everything?"

A guy goes to a fortune-teller and the fortune-teller says to him, "I'll read your palm for fifty dollars. And that entitles you to ask three questions."

And the guy asks, "Questions about what?"

And the fortune-teller says, "About anything."

And the guy asks, "Isn't fifty dollars an awful lot to charge for that?"

And the fortune-teller says, "Maybe . . . what's your last question?"

It's the revolution in Paris, the year is 1789, and three spies from England are about to be guillotined.

So the executioner says to a guy named Smith, "Do you want to be beheaded on your back or your front?" So Smith says, "On my back. I'm not afraid of death."

So Smith is laid on his back under the blade. All of a sudden the executioner pulls the lever. *Schlick*—and the blade jams. So Smith is reprieved because no man can be sentenced to death twice.

Hopkins was next. He chooses to face the blade. And again the blade jams and Hopkins gets a reprieve.

The third guy, Murphy, steps up and the executioner asks him, "Back or front?" and Murphy says, "Listen, if it's good enough for Smith and Hopkins, it's good enough for me," and Murphy lays on his back under the blade. All of a sudden he says, "Wait a minute, I think I can see why it jams!"

Bewitches The way people in Brooklyn say: "I'll be right there—I'll BEWITCHES in a second!"

Biceps Ceps that like both men and women.

Blue Jeans Tight pants that tell dirty jokes.

Bulletin Board How a bulletin feels after a conversation with Debbie Boone.

Bumble Bee Father of rock star Sting.

Butterfly A zipper on the front of a stick of margarine.

A preacher from the South arrives in New York for some meetings. He's taken to one of the biggest hotels in town and given a beautiful suite of rooms. When he walks into the bedroom, there lying on the bed with nothing on but the TV set is a beautiful girl.

Well, the preacher is livid and he gets on the phone and calls down to the front desk.

And when they answer, the preacher shouts, "What is the meaning of this outrage? How dare you embarrass me this way! I am the most distinguished clergyman in my state, and you have the audacity to humiliate me in this way! I'm going to sue this hotel for every cent it has!"

At this point the young lady gets off the bed and starts putting on her clothes. The preacher turns to her and says, "Just a moment, miss, nobody's talking to you!"

This woman wants to spend a month at a nice resort hotel but before she makes the reservation she takes the precaution of writing the hotel manager to be sure that dogs will be permitted in the hotel. So the manager gets the letter and since he has a couple of dogs, he sends her this letter:

"Dear Madam:

"I have been in the hotel business for some twenty-eight years. Never in all that time have I had to call the police to eject a disorderly dog at four o'clock in the morning. Never once has a dog set the bedclothes afire by carelessly throwing away a lighted cigarette. Never has a dog stolen my towels, bedspreads, or silverware. Of course, your dog is welcome at my hotel."

And it's signed, "Sincerely, The Manager."

And at the bottom of the letter is a P.S. and it says, "If the dog will vouch for you, you can come, too!"

There's an old drunk sitting at a bar next to a man and his wife.

All of a sudden the old drunk lets out a thundering belch. And the couple sitting next to him are startled and rather dismayed at such behavior. So the man turns around and says to the drunk, "How dare you belch in front of my wife?" And the drunk looks up and says, "Well, I'm certainly sorry. I didn't know it was her turn!"

It's almost midnight and the rain is pouring down—it's a rainstorm and the owner of a delicatessen is about to close the door, lock up and go home when a man, dripping wet, staggers through the door, shaking a wet umbrella that's been turned inside out by the heavy wind. The wet customer says to the owner, "I'd like a bagel." And the owner says, "Okay, one bagel and what?" The guy says, "That's it, one bagel."

The owner says, "No cream cheese?"

The guy says, "No, thanks."

The owner says, "A piece of lox?"

The guy says, "No lox."

The owner says, "But a takeout cup of good hot coffee, right?"

The guy says, "No, thanks. No coffee."

The deli owner stares at the dripping stranger and says, "On a terrible night like this, you came out and walked all the way here for—one—plain—bagel?" And the guy says, "That's what *she* wants."

"She?" the deli owner says. "That explains it. *She* has to be your wife, no?" And the guy says, "Certainly it's my wife. Do you think my mother would send me out for one bagel on a godforsaken night like this?"

A guy walks into a Third Avenue bar with a dog and orders two martinis: one for himself and one for the dog. So the bartender fixes the martinis and puts them down in front of the guy and his dog.

Both of them drink the martinis, eat the olives, chew up the glasses, and then spit the stems over their shoulders.

They repeat this three times. Finally the man takes a look at the bartender, puts his arms around the dog, and says, "I bet you think we're crazy, don't you?"

And the bartender says, "I sure do. The stem's the best part!"

The sales manager of a big corporation is complaining to his secretary about one of his salesmen. "I tell you, George is so forgetful. It's a wonder he can sell anything. He never remembers anything anybody tells him. I asked him to pick up some cigarettes on his way back from lunch, and I'm not sure he'll even remember to come back!"

All of a sudden the office door flies open and in comes George, the salesman he's talking about.

And the salesman says, "You'll never guess what happened. While I was at lunch, I met Old Man Brown. He hasn't bought anything from us in five years. Well, we got to talking and by the time we reached dessert, he gave me *this* half-million-dollar order!"

The sales manager turns to his secretary and says, "See, he forgot the cigarettes!"

A husband goes for a drive with his wife. And she's a typical backseat driver.

And everything he does, she complains about. "Go to the left! Go to the right! Watch that car in front, watch that car in the back! Look out for that truck! Slow down—step on the gas! Pass the sucker on the right!" She's driving him nuts.

They come to a railroad crossing and a train is bearing down on them. The guy drives halfway across the tracks and stops and jumps out of the car.

His wife hollers, "What are you doing?"

And the guy says, "I got *my* end over. What are you going to do with yours?"

There's a man waiting for his car in a garage and he's watching a mechanic working on another car. And the mechanic changes the oil without spilling a drop. And he lifts the hood and checks the water level and lowers the hood carefully and locks it. He then cleans the windshield and wipes all the greasy finger marks off the hood, checks the battery, and after washing his hands, drives the car slowly out to the street.

And the man watching all this turns to the shop foreman and says, "Now, there's a real mechanic. Look how careful he is of that car."

And the foreman says, "Yeah, it's his!"

Carport Cheap wine you drink when you drive.

Chestnuts People who are crazy about Dolly Parton.

Chinese Checkers Income tax auditors in Peking. (Also, supermarket cashiers in Hong Kong.)

Cognac What a Yak puts ice cream in.

A father says to his wife, "We're going to find out what Tommy wants to be when he grows up. Watch this."

He puts a ten-dollar bill on the table and he says, "This represents a banker." Next to it, he places a brand new Bible. "This," he says, "represents a clergyman," and beside the Bible, he places a bottle of whiskey. And the father says, "This represents a bum!"

So then the two of them hide where they can see the articles on the table. Pretty soon the kid comes into the room, whistling, and spies the objects on the table. He looks around to see if he's alone. He doesn't see anyone, so he picks up the ten-spot, holds it to the light, and puts it down. Then he fingers through the Bible as he walks around again. Then he quickly uncorks the bottle and smells the contents. And then in one quick motion, he picks up the bill and stuffs it in his pocket, puts the Bible under his arm, grabs the bottle, and walks out of the room whistling.

The father then turns to his wife and says, "How about that? My God, he's going to be a politician!"

A young married couple lives in an apartment next door to a model, and whenever the guy goes over to borrow something, his wife notices that it takes him longer than she thinks is necessary.

One day he goes over to borrow a cup of sugar and is gone half an hour. So the guy's wife pounds on the wall several times and gets no answer. Finally, she goes to the phone and calls next door.

And she says to the model, "I would like to know why it takes my husband so long to get anything when he goes over there!"

And the model says, "I'll tell you one thing. All these interruptions certainly aren't helping!"

There are these two bums who are on the highway looking for a ride and after waiting in the hot sun for two hours they start walking down the road.

As they pass an old house they see an old motorcycle with a sidecar parked under a tree out in front. They look at each other and they run over to the motorcycle and get in and drive off, leaving a cloud of dust.

After about half an hour the driver looks at his friend in the sidecar and jams on the brakes.

The bum in the sidecar is having trouble. His face is red, his eyes are protruding, and he can hardly breathe. So the driver says, "What's the matter?"

And the other bum in the sidecar says, "I'll tell you what's the matter. There's no bottom in this thing and I've been running trying to keep up with you!"

Two partners were both going with their secretary. One day she comes in and tells them that she's pregnant.

Each one of them blames the other. One of the partners goes on a trip and while he's away the secretary goes to the hospital. Soon after, one of the partners sends his partner, who's on a trip, a telegram that says:

"SALLY GAVE BIRTH TO TWINS—MINE DIED."

A guy checks out of his hotel room and he discovers that he has forgotten his umbrella. By the time he goes back to his room, the hotel has rented the room to a young honeymoon couple. So the guy, before he knocks, hears a wild conversation going on inside the room.

"Whose little hair is this?"
"All yours, honey."
"Whose little eyes are these?"
"All yours, honey."
"And whose little nose is this?"
"All yours, honey."
"And whose little mouth is this?"
"All yours, honey."

And the guy, standing outside, can't contain himself any longer, and yells through the door, "When you come to an umbrella, that's mine!"

A guy is barreling a big aluminum-sided truck down the highway at breakneck speeds. All of a sudden he pulls the truck over to the side of the road and gets out with a crowbar in his hands. And then he proceeds to run around the truck hitting it with the crowbar. Then he gets back in the truck and drives on down the road.

After a couple of miles down the highway the trucker repeats the same ceremony. He gets out of the aluminum truck and again spends ten minutes running around the truck beating the sides with the crowbar. After he finishes he again gets into the truck and pulls out on the highway again. Ten miles down the road the truck pulls off on the side and again the trucker gets out and again runs around the rig beating it with the crowbar. As he's getting back into the driver's seat, a guy approaches him and says, "I've been following you down this highway for an hour and you've been pulling off the side of the road and beating big dents in your truck. What in the hell is going on?" So the driver says, "Well, the load limit on this highway is five thousand pounds. I've got ten thousand pounds of canaries in there. I've got to keep half of them flying all the time!"

A couple are in bed and the girl snuggles up to the guy and they pull the bed sheets up around their chins.

And the girl says, "Darling, how many others were there before me?"

After a few minutes of silence, the girl says with a small pout on her face, "Well, I'm waiting."

And the guy takes a puff on his cigarette and says, "Well, I'm still counting!"

There's an Irish priest who had worked so hard in his church that he was getting terribly mixed up over a lot of problems concerning his parish. So he goes to a psychiatrist who tells him to forget his parish and his flock and go to London and enjoy himself for a few days. As he leaves the doctor's office the psychiatrist says to him, "Take your dog collar off and let your hair down."

So the priest decides to do that and he goes to London, takes off his dog collar, sees a movie, goes to a nice restaurant, and has a few drops of the hard stuff.

Later that night he finds himself in Soho, in one of the clip joints. He no sooner sits down at a table and a topless waitress comes up and says, "What would you like to drink, Father?" The priest panics, thinking he must have left his collar on, and stutters out, "How did you know I was a priest?" And the waitress says, "Oh, I'm Sister Theresa. I go to the same psychiatrist."

A middle-aged guy goes to his doctor and tells him that his wife is always nagging him about his vanishing potency.

So the doctor gives him a bottle of pills and tells him that these pills will work wonders. A month later the guy goes back to the doctor and he's happy.

"The pills are terrific," the guy says. "I've been making love three times a night." And the doctor says, "That's wonderful. What does your wife say about your lovemaking now?"

And the guy says, "I don't know. I haven't been home yet!"

A pregnant woman tells her husband he'd better get her to the hospital. So right away the nervous husband runs to the phone and calls the hospital.

He tells them he's bringing his wife in and they should notify everybody that she is going to have a baby.

And the receptionist asks, "Is this her first baby?"

And the guy says, "Of course not. This is her husband!"

Cold Tablet   What an Eskimo writes notes on.

Debate   In Brooklyn, what you use to catch de fish with—de bate.

Defrost   What gets on de windshield after a cold night.

Dialogue   How you make a phone call to a tree.

Two men, both of them good friends and both of them ready for retirement at the end of the year, are working at a plant and one of them says to the other, "Last night I made love to my wife three times." And his friend says, "Three times? How did you do it?"

And his friend says, "It was easy. I made love to my wife, then I rolled over and took a ten-minute nap. I woke up, I made love to my wife again, then rolled over and took another nap for ten minutes. I woke up, made love to my wife again and then I went to sleep. I woke up feeling like a teenager again."

So his friend says, "Wow, that's fantastic. I'm going to give that a try!" So he goes home that night and goes to bed. He makes love to his wife and then rolls over and takes a nap for ten minutes. He wakes up, makes love to his wife and rolls over and takes a ten-minute nap. He wakes up, makes love to his wife the third time and falls asleep. He wakes up in the morning and he's twenty minutes late for work. He throws on his clothes and runs down to the factory. When he gets there, the boss is waiting. The guy says, "Boss, I've been working for you twenty years and I've never been late before. You've got to forgive me these twenty minutes this time!" And the boss says, "What twenty minutes? Where were you Tuesday, where were you Wednesday?"

One guy at the country club is beating everybody on the golf course. He's a big strapping guy and he really hits the golf ball! Not only did he have all the other guys down about losing but he bragged about how good he was. Finally, one of the golfers got an idea. Seems he had read somewhere that an animal trainer had taught a gorilla how to play golf. So the guy calls up the trainer and makes a deal to bring the gorilla to the club. The guy asks the trainer, "Now, is this gorilla really that good?" And the trainer says, "Good? He can hit a golf ball 450 yards!"

So the next day the gorilla shows up and the match is set up with the club champion. The gorilla picks up a driver and tees off, and true to the claims, the ball sails 450 yards through the air and drops four inches from the cup. The club champ is dumbfounded and in shock. The other players are ecstatic and jumping up and down with joy. The caddy then hands the gorilla a putter. The gorilla swings and hits the ball 450 yards!!!

Two businessmen were having lunch and they started talking about world problems, high taxes, the cost of living, their families.

And one of them says very proudly, "I have six boys."

So the other guy says, "That's a nice family. I wish to heaven I had six children."

And the proud father says with a touch of sympathy in his voice, "Don't you have any children?"

And the other guy says, "Yeah, ten!"

One day a gate breaks down between heaven and hell. So St. Peter arrives on the scene and calls out for the devil. And the devil saunters over and says, "What do you want?" And St. Peter says, "Satan, it's your turn to fix it this time."

And the devil says, "I'm sorry. But my men are too busy to worry about fixing a mere gate."

And St. Peter says, "Well, then, I'll have to sue you for breaking our agreement."

And the devil says, "Oh, yeah? Where you going to get a lawyer?"

One day a precocious teenager returns home late from school and confesses to his mother that he had made love to his girlfriend. So his mother says, "I'm really disappointed in you. But for telling me the truth, you can do down to the corner drugstore for a milkshake."

The next day the kid comes home late again and this time confesses to making love to one of the neighbors' wives. So his mother says, "Well, at least you're still honest." And again he's rewarded with a milkshake.

On the third day the boy casually strolls into the house and announces to both of his parents that he had stayed after school and made love to his teacher.

As his mother starts to scold him, the father picks up a frying pan. The mother jumps up and screams, "Don't hit him! At least he told the truth!"

And the father hollers, "Hit him? Hell, I'm going to cook him a steak. How long do you expect him to keep this up on those lousy milkshakes?"

An eighty-year-old widowed grandfather surprises everyone at Sunday dinner over at his granddaughter's when he shows up with his new bride, a petite redhead.

When everyone at the table learns that the new bride is just nineteen, they explode with astonishment and, bewildered, they take the elderly gentleman aside and say, "Grandfather, how could you do something so outrageous as this? Marrying a nineteen-year-old girl. You're over eighty. Do you realize that sex with a young girl like that at your age could be fatal?"

And the old man looks at them and says, "If she dies, she dies—so I'll get another one!"

It's a hot day—there's a traveling salesman passing through a small town in Texas when he sees a little old man sitting in a rocking chair on the porch of a house. So he stops and says to the little old man, "You don't look as if you have a care in the world. What's your formula for a long and happy life?"

And the little old man says, "Well, I smoke six packs of cigarettes a day, I drink a quart of bourbon every four hours and six cases of beer a week. I never wash and I go out every night; I don't get to bed until four in the morning."

And the guy says, "Wow, that's just great. How old are you?"

And the little man says, "Twenty-two!"

An advertising executive complains to his commuter friend that he can't seem to meet any ladies. So his friend says to him, "I'll give you a good tip. This afternoon, take the train to Westport. When you get there, you'll see a lot of good-looking ladies waiting in their cars. Some of them will be disappointed because their husbands missed the train and they'll be very vulnerable. You go up to them, explain that you were expecting someone to meet you, and you strike up a conversation. From there on, who knows what can happen."

So the guy goes to Grand Central and boards a train. After it pulls out of the station, the guy realizes it doesn't stop at Westport. Instead, it stops in Greenwich and he figures the same tactics will work there.

Sure enough, in Greenwich there's a beautiful woman who's disappointed her husband hasn't shown up. So the guy strikes up a conversation with her and pretty soon the woman invites him back to her house for a drink and then one thing leads to another.

An hour later her husband shows up and finds them in bed. So the guy screams at his wife, "How could you do this to me?" And then he turns to the guy in bed and says, "And you, you stupid idiot, I told you to get off at Westport!"

It's Friday and it's payday, so when this guy, who's a driller on an offshore rig, gets his check cashed, the first thing he does is head for the nearest gambling joint. He first drinks a shot of booze with a beer chaser and saunters over to the dice table.

He lays out a hundred-dollar bet and shakes the dice and lets them fly down the table. But as he throws them, a third dice falls from his sleeve.

Everybody stops cold and the dealer picks up the dice, pockets one of them, and hands two of them back to the driller and says, "Okay, roll again. Your point is fifteen!"

An eighty-year-old woman goes to the doctor for a complete physical examination and the doctor says, "You're in perfect health."

And the doctor gets ready to see her to the door and the woman says, "Could you give me a prescription for some birth control pills?"

And the doctor says, "Birth control pills? For what?"

And the woman says, "To get rid of my headache."

And the doctor says, "To get rid of your headache?"

And the woman says, "Yes. I live with my granddaughter, a lovely twenty-three-year-old girl. Every morning we get up and have breakfast together. When she's not looking I take the birth control pill and put it in her coffee—it gets rid of my headache!"

An excited woman calls the police station one day and says to the officer on the phone, "There's an enormous gray animal in my garden pulling up cabbages with his tail."

And the officer says, "What's he doing with them?"

And the woman says, "If I told you, you'd never believe me."

A guy is at a cocktail party. He spots a good-looking girl standing by herself and walks over to her and says, "How about us going off in a corner and doing a little 'kissie face'?" And the girl says, "That'll be the day."

Then the guy says, "Okay, then, how about us going up to my apartment and doing a little loving?" And the girl takes a sip from her drink and says, "That'll be the day." And the guy says, "Well, then, how about us taking my private jet and spending the weekend at my château in France?"

And the girl takes another drink and says, *"This'll* be the day!"

There's this big movie star, who has always done his own stunts, who decides it is time to get a stand-in, or in this case a double, and hits on the novel idea of getting a clone of himself.

So, secretly, and at great cost, he has it done and the plan is a great success as the clone takes all the risks and bruises.

However, one day the actor is surprised when the clone bursts into his penthouse apartment swearing and yelling at him. The actor tries to calm the clone, but to no avail. Finally the clone becomes so agitated that he physically attacks the actor. The actor fights back and manages to cause the other man to fall off the penthouse balcony to his death.

Ten minutes later the police arrive and tell the actor that he's under arrest. And the actor says, "Arrest me for what? That wasn't a real person so the murder charge won't hold up in court. Just try and charge me."

So the police think for a moment and one of them says to the actor, "Oh, yeah? I've got it. *We're charging you with making an obscene clone fall!*"

Dish Soap   As opposed to . . . dat soap.

Duran Duran   The Mayor of Walla Walla.

Eyelashes   Windshield wipers for contact lenses.

A woman who has just finished a first-aid course is walking down the street and she sees a man lying face down in a flooded gutter.

So she rushes over to him, turns him on his back, and begins to give him mouth-to-mouth resuscitation.

Suddenly the guy sits up and pushes the woman away and says, "I don't know what you have on your mind, lady, but I'm supposed to be clearing this drain!"

A mother calls her daughter on the phone and asks how she's feeling.

And all she hears for five minutes is, "I feel terrible. My head's splitting, my back and legs are killing me. The house is a mess and the kids are driving me up a wall!"

So the mother says, "Listen, go lie down. I'll be right over and I'll cook some lunch for you, clean the house, and take the kids out while you get some rest. By the way, how's Harold?"

And the woman says, "Harold?"

And the mother says, "Yes. Harold, your husband."

And the woman says, "My husband isn't named Harold."

And the other lady says, "Good gosh, I must have dialed the wrong number!"

And then the younger woman says, "Does that mean you're not coming over?"

There's this guy who's groggy from lack of sleep and his friends start to worry about him because he's walking into walls. So a friend of his says to him, "Come on, you've got to get hold of yourself. Stop staying up and worrying. It's over, get on with it." He says, "I know your wife left you, but don't let it get you down. *You've got to get some sleep.* Why don't you try counting sheep?"

And the guy says, "I don't have time, I'm too busy counting my lucky stars!"

A drunk gets on the crosstown bus and staggers up the aisle, bumping into passengers, and finally plops into a seat beside a little old lady.

She looks at him up and down, sniffs, and says, "I've got news for you. You're going straight to hell!"

And the drunk jumps up and says, "Good heavens, I'm on the wrong bus!"

A guy goes to a skydiver's school and becomes a skydiver, and then he goes for instructions on how to use the parachute.

So the instructor tells him, "You count to ten and pull the ripcord."

And the skydiver says, "W-w-w-w-what w-w-w-w-was th-th-th-th-the nu-nu-nu-number a-a-ag-gain?"

And the instructor says, "Three!"

A famous art collector is walking through Greenwich Village when he notices a mangy old cat lapping milk from a saucer in front of a store. And the collector does a double take when he sees the saucer. He knows it's very old and very valuable. So he saunters casually into the store and offers to buy the cat for two dollars.

But the store owner says to him, "I'm sorry, but the cat isn't for sale."

And the collector says, "Please. I need a hungry old tom cat around the house to catch mice. I'll give you ten dollars for him."

And the owner says, "Sold," and takes the ten dollars.

The the collector says, "Listen, I was wondering if, for the ten dollars, you might include that old saucer. The cat seems to be used to it. It'll save me a dish."

And the owner says, "Sorry, buddy. That's my lucky saucer. So far this week, I've sold sixty-eight cats!"

A guy is told by his doctor that he's got to stop drinking. And he tells him that every time he feels like taking a drink, he should eat something. So he tries it, and finds out that it works. Every time he wants a drink, he just eats something.

One night while stopping at a hotel, he hears a strange sound in the next room and he walks out of his room and the door to the room next to his is open and there's a man just about to hang himself.

So he runs down the stairs three steps at a time and he runs up to the clerk behind the counter and says, "There's a feller in the next room, the room next to mine, he's hanging himself! For God's sake, give me a plate of ham and eggs!"

A guy has a blind date with a girl a friend fixes him up with. So to impress the girl, the guy takes her to one of New York's finest restaurants.

When the captain asks her what she'd like for dinner, the wisp of a girl starts to order and makes her date sit up as he mentally figures up the cost of the meal.

The girl continues to order. "And after the filet mignon and the fresh asparagus, I'll have a lobster, crêpes Suzette, and some of your finest imported cheese."

Then she turns to the guy and asks, "What do you suggest I wash it down with?"

And the guy says, "How about the Hudson River?"

A little man is praying. "Please, you know me. I'm always praying to you and yet I have had nothing but bad luck, misery, sickness, and despair all my life—and look at the butcher next door—he's never prayed in his life—just look at him. He has nothing but prosperity, health, and joy. How come a believer like me is always in trouble and *he* is always doing good?"

And suddenly a voice booms out, "Because the butcher isn't always bugging me—that's why!"

! ¡ !

A guy in Atlantic City gambles away every last cent and he's forced to borrow a dime to use the restroom pay toilet.

When he gets to the men's room he finds an unlocked stall and he knows he has one last dime to use in a slot machine. So he uses the dime, hits the jackpot, and parlays that jackpot into millions of dollars.

So now that he's rich and famous, he goes on a lecture tour telling his story and then declares that if he ever finds his benefactor he will split his fortune with him.

After he's given his lecture a few thousand times, a man jumps up one night at a lecture and shouts, "I'm him. I'm the man who gave you the dime for the toilet!" And the lucky gambler hollers back, "You're not the one. I'm looking for the guy who left the door open!"

There's a guy working at a sawmill and one day he pushes a log through the saw and, not paying any attention, shaves off all ten of his fingers.

So he rushes to the hospital and runs into the emergency room to see a doctor.

So the doctor says to him, "I'll see what I can do. Give me the fingers."

And the workman says to the doctor, "I haven't got the fingers!" And the doctor says, "What? In this day of modern technology and microsurgery, we could probably put them all back on and make you good as new! Why didn't you bring the fingers?"

And the guy looks at the doctor and says, "Bring 'em? Hell, Doc, I couldn't pick 'em up!"

Two fathers are at a PTA meeting and they're discussing their families.

One of the fathers says, "Now, my three boys sure stick together. They're the Three Musketeers, Curly, Larry, and Moe. They're always together. When one of them gets in trouble, the other two will never squeal on him."

And the other dad says, "That's something great, but tell me, how do you find out the guilty one so that you can punish him?"

And the other father says, "Oh, that's easy. All I do is send all three of them to bed without supper, and the next morning I beat the hell out of the one with the black eye."

Hip Huggers   Overly friendly midgets.

Englebert Humperdinck   That's what people in Scandinavia say after a heavy meal.

Information   What airplanes fly in (*in formation*).

Iran   What I did when a mugger chased me. . . . I Ran.

Jockey Shorts   What happens when you don't wire Willie Shoemaker properly.

Elton John   Expensive bathroom fixture in Hugh Hefner's mansion.

There's a flood in a little Ohio town and a little girl and a small boy are sitting on top of a house.

As they sit there watching different articles floating along the water, they notice a derby hat float by. Pretty soon the hat turns and comes back and then it turns again and goes downstream. After it goes some distance, it again turns around and comes back.

So the little girl says, "Do you see that derby? First it goes downstream. And then it turns and comes back."

And the little boy says, "Oh, that's my father. This morning he said come hell or high water, he was going to cut the grass today!"

A guy is meeting the President in the Oval Office and he sees all these phones on the President's desk. So he asks the President what each one is for. So the President says, "You see this red one. This connects me directly to the Premier in Moscow. And this white one here is my direct line to God."

And the guy says, "Golly, a direct line to God! How much does a call to God cost?"

And the President says, "Oh, it's about a thousand dollars a minute."

So the guy leaves and he's really impressed.

A couple of months later the same guy happens to visit the Prime Minister of Israel in the leader's office. And he sees a bunch of phones on the Prime Minister's desk and he asks him about the different phones. So the Prime Minister says, "This blue phone is a direct line to the President of the United States, this red phone is a direct line to the Premier of the U.S.S.R." And the Minister says, "You know, it costs me two hundred dollars a minute to speak to the Russian Premier." And the guy says, "That's a lot of money." And then the guy adds, "But what is that white phone there?" And the Prime Minister says, "Oh, that's my direct line to God." "And how much does it cost you?" the guy asks. And the Prime Minister says, "Twenty-five cents." And the guy says, "Twenty-five cents? When I was with the *President* he told me it cost *him* a thousand dollars to talk to God!" And the Prime Minister says, "Well, you see, from *here*, it's a local call!"

A guy gets a flat tire in front of an asylum. And as he takes the wheel off, the bolts that hold the wheel roll down the sewer.

An inmate of the asylum watching all of this says to the motorist, "Listen, just take one bolt from the other three tires to hold the fourth wheel in place until you can get to the gas station."

So the motorist says to him, "Thanks a lot. I don't know why you're in that place."

And the inmate says, "I'm here for being crazy—not for being stupid!"

A woman goes to a séance in hopes that she'll be able to communicate with the spirit of her late husband.

So the medium, holding hands with the rest of the group in a circle, goes into a deep trance, and after a while a voice says, "Gladys, is that you?"

And the widow says, "Harold, I'd know your voice anywhere. How are you?"

And the voice says, "Fine!"

And the widow says, "How is it there? Where are you?"

And the voice of her husband says, "Wonderful. Today the sky is deep blue, the temperature is perfect, and the grass is deep and high. And the cows are everywhere—beautiful cows of every color."

And his wife says, "Isn't that amazing? I had no idea there'd be cows in heaven." And her husband says, "Heaven? Who's talking about heaven? I'm a bull in Minnesota!"

A guy goes to his doctor to find out how his physical examination turned out.

And the doctor says, "I've got some bad news for you. You've got six months to live."

And the guy says, "Oh, my God, what am I going to do?"

And the doctor says, "If I were you I'd move to Cleveland and get married."

And the guy says, "If I do that, will I live longer than six months?"

And the doctor says, "No, but it'll seem like it!"

An Earth couple is carried away to Mars by a Martian spaceship. After landing they're told that no harm will be done to them, but the only reason they were abducted was to study them.

So after a cordial day of questioning, the Martian leader says, "I think we're just about done with you, but we have one final request."

And the Earth couple ask what it is and the Martian says, "Could you show us how you get your babies?"

Well, after much self-conscious hemming and hawing, the couple decide that they should perform for the sake of interplanetary understanding.

When they're finished, the Martian leader says, "How disappointing!"

And the couple says in unison, "Disappointing? Why?"

And the Martian says, "Because that's how *we* make automobiles!"

A wealthy farmer goes to church on Sunday and listens to the reverend deliver one of his sermons.

After church the farmer stands in line to congratulate the reverend on a fine sermon.

And he says to the reverend, "That was a damn good sermon, damn good!"

And the minister is pleased, but he's a little shocked and says, "It would be nicer if you didn't use such language to express yourself."

And the farmer says, "I can't help it, Reverend— but I still think it was a damn good sermon—that's why I put five hundred dollars in the collection basket."

And the minister says, "The hell you did!"

There was a girl who lived alone in New York City and asked her boyfriend to buy her a pet for Christmas that would keep her company.

So the guy found a beautiful yellow canary which sang light opera but unfortunately had only one leg.

Now, the girl loved the bird's voice but she couldn't bear to look at the poor thing standing on one leg. So she asked her boyfriend if he'd trade it in for a whole bird.

So the next day the guy takes the canary back to the pet shop and tells the owner that his girl loves the bird but she can't bear to see such a pathetic creature on only one leg.

So the guy says, "If you don't mind, I'd like to trade this one in for a bird with two legs!"

And the pet store owner says, "Whaddya want, a singer or a dancer!"

Kent Jewish word for *can't.*

Kidney The area just above the shin on a child.

Lawsuit What a lawyer wears to court.

Linguine An Italian who speaks several languages.

Marlboro A donkey who lives in the village of Marl.

A guy goes into a cafeteria and gets some custard pie and goes over to a table. He's about to sit down and he realizes he's forgotten to get coffee.

So he puts the pie down and goes for coffee. When he returns to his table a man is sitting there.

So the guy says, "That's my seat, you've got my chair!"

And the man says, "What do you mean, your chair? How do you know it's your chair?"

And the guy says, "Because you're sitting on my custard pie!"

A big automobile manufacturer was so knocked out about the assembly lines, he advertised that in a test one of his cars had been put together in exactly six minutes.

So the next day he receives a phone call from a guy who says, "Is that advertisement about assembling a car in six minutes true?"

And the manufacturer says to him, "Yes, sir, an automobile was actually turned out in precisely that time."

And the other guy on the phone says, "Well, I just wanted to know. I think I'm the owner of that car!"

A man takes his wife to the Bronx Zoo and while they're standing in front of the gorilla cage, the man turns to his wife and says, "Listen, honey, take off your clothes. I want to see how the big ape reacts."

And his wife says, "Are you out of your mind?"

And the guy says, "There's no one around. Come on, take off your clothes. I want to see what the gorilla does."

So the woman reluctantly starts taking off her clothes and the gorilla starts jumping up and down and running back and forth in the cage. When she finally undresses, the ape goes wild. He starts making noises, beating his chest, jumping up and down, and he starts rattling the bars of the cage.

With this, the man opens the door to the cage, shoves his wife in, closes the door and says, "*Now*, I want you to tell *him* you have a headache!"

A skydiver jumps out of a plane and when it comes time to pull the ripcord, nothing happens. So then he mutters, "I still have my emergency chute." So he pulls the ripcord and again, nothing happens. The skydiver says to himself, "I'm a goner!"

All of a sudden he sees a man flying up from Earth toward him.

When the man gets close enough to him, the skydiver hollers down, "Hey, do you know anything about parachutes?"

And the guy coming up hollers back, "No! Do you know anything about gas stoves?"

A guy is standing in front of his locker at the country club admiring a golf ball he has in his hand. One of his golfing buddies says to him, "What'd you do, get some new golf balls?"

And the guy says, "Would you believe that this is the greatest golf ball ever made. You can't lose it. You hit it into the rough and it whistles. You hit it in the woods and a bell inside goes off. If you drive it into a lake, a big burst of steam shoots up six feet in the air for two minutes."

And his friend says, "That's great. Where did you get it?"

And the guy says, "I found it!"

There's this family and they have an eight-year-old boy who has never spoken a word. And like any parents with a situation like this, they are worried sick. One morning while the three of them are having breakfast the boy looks up and says, "Could I have a little more sugar on my cereal?"

The parents look at each other. They're dumbfounded. They rush to each other and start crying hysterically and they pick up the little boy and they dance around the kitchen crying with joy. And the mother breaks down, crying, "You spoke. You said something! Tell us, why have you waited all these years?"

And the little kid shrugs his shoulders and says, "Up till this, everything's been okay!"

A bookkeeper goes into the manager's office with a big smile on his face and says, "Hey, boss! You remember that big Christmas order we got from the Palace Company?"

And the manager says, "Of course I do, what about it?"

The bookkeeper says, "That was the order that finally put us in the black."

And the boss says, "Wonderful. Now you can throw out that damn bottle of red ink and run out and get a bottle of black."

And the bookkeeper says, "I can't do that. If I went out and bought a bottle of black ink, we would be in the red again."

A traveling salesman stops in a country store to buy a bottle of soda pop. As he starts to take a drink he looks over to the other side of the store and sees four men playing poker with a fox terrier.

He walks over to the game and stands there mesmerized as he watches the dog call for two cards, raise his bet, and rake in the pot.

Finally, the salesman says to one of the guys at the table, "That's amazing. I've never seen such a smart dog in all my life!"

And one of the guys at the table looks up and says, "He ain't smart. Whenever he gets a real good hand he wags his tail!"

A six-year-old boy sits down at the dinner table with his mother and father. So his dad asks him what he did today and he says that he played soccer in the backyard and proposed to his friend Susie who lives next door.

So his father, going along with the situation, says, "Well, you're six and Susie is five. What are you all going to do about expenses?"

And the boy says, "Well, I figured with the fifty cents I get for allowance and with the fifty cents Susie gets from her parents, we'll get along fine."

So his parents laugh and his father says, "Yes, but what'll you do when you have children?"

And the kid says, "Well, up till now we've been lucky!"

A guy named Kramer is in the hospital a long time. One night the phone rings at the night nurse's table. And she says, "Hello," and the voice says, "Could you tell me how Mr. Kramer is doing?" And the nurse says, "He's doing very well; as a matter of fact, he's being discharged tomorrow." And the voice says, "Thank you," and the nurse says, "Who shall I say called?" And the voice says, "This is Mr. Kramer—the doctors don't tell me a damn thing!"

There was an unsuccessful politician, poor but honest. One day he goes to his ward leader and says, "I have thirty votes in my family and I control two hundred more, why can't I be an Assemblyman?"

So after a little persuasion, the leader ran him for office and he was elected.

Two years later the guy comes back and requests that they run him for Congress and the ward leader grants his request and the guy is elected. Four years later the guy asks to run for Governor and again the leader consents and again the guy wins.

Not too long afterward, the guy comes back to the boss and says, "You've got to do me another favor!"

So the head politician starts screaming, "I don't believe you. I made you an Assemblyman. I made you a Congressman and I made you Governor. What do you want me to do now? Make you President?"

And the Governor says, "No. Make me a citizen!"

There's this noisy convention going on in Chicago and the master of ceremonies is trying to settle down the house before introducing the singer who's the star of the evening.

Finally, one of the officials jumps up to the stage, grabs the mike, and hollers, "Okay, youse guys, shut up and let the man work!"

Everyone quiets down and from a side entrance, suddenly the singer comes out singing at the top of his lungs, "Feelings, nothing more than feelings," and without a word of warning, a fist crashes into his face and an indignant trucker says, "You heard the boss. Shut up!"

!

There's a smart young man working in the produce section of a large supermarket and a big mean-looking customer interrupts him and says, "I'd like a half a head of lettuce."

And the young clerk looks at the guy and says, "Sir, we can't sell half a head of lettuce."

But the customer, who's a big burly guy, insists, so the clerk tells him he'll check with the store's manager.

He finds the store manager and says, "Mr. Abernathy, there's some blithering idiot in the produce department who wants to buy half a head of lettuce." Just as he finishes his statement he turns and sees that the customer has followed him and is standing right in back of him. So the young clerk turns back to the store manager and says, "And this gentleman wants to buy the other half."

Only the guys on the Mets team will give you a smile and shake their heads about an incident that happened last month at Shea Stadium.

One afternoon a horse wandered onto the field up to Davey Johnson and said, "Why don't you use me on your team? I can hit and field as well as anyone on your team."

But Davey Johnson says, "Get lost, I've got enough troubles." And the horse says, "Come on, Davey, give me a chance—try me in the field."

So, figuring it'll be good for a few laughs, Davey says, "Okay, just for laughs, though." So the horse goes into the outfield and makes one great catch after another. So Davey says, "Okay, come on in and bat." So the horse gets into the batting cage and hits one ball after another over the fence. So they play an intrasquad game and the first three batters are put out by the dazzling fielding of the horse. When the horse's team (the team he's playing for, that is) comes to bat, they load up the bases and the horse gets up to bat. He blasts the first ball over the Shea Stadium fence and the horse just stands there. So Davey Johnson yells, "Run, run!" And the horse looks over to the dugout and says, "If I could run, I'd be racing at Aqueduct!"

Migraine   A possessive farmer talking about his wheat.

Monkeys   What they use to unlock the doors in a monastery.

The bell captain at the St. Moritz gets a phone call from a guest in the wee hours. The guy says to the captain, "What time does the hotel bar open?"

And the bell captain says, "It opens at ten A.M., sir."

An hour later, the same guy calls back and he asks the bell captain again, "What time does the hotel bar open?" And the bell captain tells him again, "The bar opens at ten A.M., sir!" and hangs up.

Two hours later, the bell captain gets another call from the same guy. And again the guy asks the bell captain, "What time does the hotel bar open?" And now the captain is getting bugged and he says to the guy, "Look, sir, I'm not going to tell you again. There's no way you can get in the bar until ten!" And the guy says, "Get in? I want to get out!"

A guy with a dog act shows up on Broadway and walks into a theatrical booking office.

After a lot of talking, begging, and pleading, the booking agent agrees to look at the act.

So the guy walks into the agent's office with a toy poodle and a Great Dane. And the toy poodle walks to the middle of the office floor and announces to the agent that he would like to tell him a few jokes.

The poodle starts telling jokes and the agent jumps up and says, "Wow, that poodle is sensational!"

And the owner says, "No. The poodle is nothing. The Great Dane is a ventriloquist!"

There once was this little snail who loved fast sports cars. So he bought himself a red Porsche, and painted a big black *S* on each door.

One day while going down the highway at a hundred miles per hour, he was spotted by a state trooper, who said to his partner, "Brother, look at that S-car go!"

A drunk telephones the police station one night and he tells the desk sergeant that he wants to report a robbery. He says, "Man, they stole the steering wheel, the brake pedal, the accelerator, the clutch pedal, and the dashboard!"

And the sergeant takes down all the information and says, "Don't you worry, we're going to investigate this as soon as I hang up."

And no sooner does he hang up than the phone rings again. The sergeant says, "Yeah." And the guy who had just called says, "Hey, don't bother. I got in the back seat by mistake!"

A little boy is sitting on the curb crying and an old man walks by. He sees the little boy sobbing and goes over to him and says, "What's the matter, little boy? Why are you crying?"

And the little boy looks up and says, "I'm crying because I can't do what the big boys do."

So the old man sat down on the curb and cried too.

A racehorse owner decides to sell his racehorse very cheap even though the horse has won several races.

When a prospective buyer shows up to look at the horse, the owner says, "Yes, I've had Irving for a while now, but he's too much of a ham. He thinks he's an actor. When he won a race by four lengths, he sneered at the other horses. Last week in a photo finish, he turned his head so the camera could get his good side."

So the buyer says, "I don't care if he wants to be an actor. I'll take him anyway. Here's your money."

So the ex-owner puts the money in his pocket and leads the buyer to the stable. When he gets to the horse, he says, "Irving, this is your new owner. Get up and do your lame impression!"

It's an old, seedy, rundown gymnasium on the lower West Side catering to young and old boxers. Amidst the yelling, the smell of fighters, sweating, punching bags and each other, one of the boxers comes over to his corner following three rounds of heavy hitting and says to his manager, "I really want a shot at the kid, Kid Jackson. I know I'm getting old and a little punchy, but before I retire I just want one chance in the ring with him!"

And the manager, wiping the fighter's face with a towel, says, "Look, if I've told you once, I've told you a hundred times: *You're* Kid Jackson!"

A little girl walks into her mother's bedroom at three o'clock in the morning. And she wakes up her mother saying, "Tell me a story, Mommy."

And her mother says, "For heaven's sake, it's three o'clock in the morning."

And the little girl says, "Please, Mommy, tell me a story."

And her mother rises up in bed and says, "Why don't you wait until four o'clock when your father comes home and he'll tell us both a story!"

A young man goes to a psychologist to take some personality tests.

So the psychologist draws a vertical line and says to the young guy, "What does this make you think of?"

And the young man says, "Sex."

So the psychologist draws a circle on the paper and shows it to the guy. And the doctor says, "And what does this make you think of?"

And the young guy says, "Sex."

Then the doctor draws a star and says, "And what about this?"

And the guy says, "Sex."

And with that, the psychologist puts his pencil down on the desk and says, "In my opinion, you have an obsession about sex."

And the young man jumps up from his chair and says, "*I* have an obsession? Who's drawing all the dirty pictures?"

A farmer and his wife take three of their pigs over to a neighboring farmer to get them mated. While the pigs are mating, the farmer asks, "How will we know if the mating is a success?" And the farmer with the pigs is told that if the pigs "eat grass," that means it's a success. If not, they'll roll around in the mud.

So after a few days the farmer comes down for breakfast and asks his wife, "Are they eating grass or rolling around in the mud?" And his wife says, "They're rolling around in the mud." So they put the three pigs in the car and take them back to the neighboring farm to get them mated again. After a couple of days, the farmer again comes down to breakfast and asks his wife, "What are they doing?" And again the farmer's wife says, "They're rolling around in the mud." So the farmer is angry and frustrated and says, "I've got a lot of work to do and I don't have time to keep doing this, but let's get them in the car and take them back over again." So again they take the three pigs back to the neighboring farmer and have them mated again.

Three days go by and the farmer comes down to breakfast and says to his wife, "Are they eating grass or rolling around in the mud?" And his wife says, "Neither. Two of them are in the back seat of the car and the other one is up front honking on the horn!"

A salesman calls up a prospective customer and the phone is answered by an obviously small boy.

And the salesman says, "Is your mother or father home?" And the little boy says, "No." So the salesman says, "Well, is there anyone else there I can speak to?"

And the little boy says, "My sister." So the salesman says, "Can I speak to her?" And the little boy says, "Yes." So the salesman waits and after a long period of silence, the little boy gets back on the phone and says, "I can't lift her out of the playpen!"

There's a bus loaded with women and they're returning from a church-workers' convention. The bus overturns and all the women are killed. Now they all go to heaven and St. Peter greets them at the pearly gates and explains to them that heaven is full and that he's gonna have to put them up in hell until the new subdivision is completed.

Three weeks later the devil frantically calls Peter and begs him, "Please take these women off my hands!"

And St. Peter says, "I can't. I'm still having housing troubles!"

And the devil says, "Troubles? You don't know what trouble is! What with their cake bakes, rummage sales, and bazaars, these women are only forty dollars short of air-conditioning this place!"

There's a big business tycoon dying and the priest hasn't arrived yet.

And the dying man's partner is at bedside with him. All of a sudden the dying man in bed raises himself up, grasps his partner, and says, "I want to confess to you. I stole that seventy-four thousand dollars from the safe. And I'm the one who told your wife about your mistress. And John—I sold our secret patents to our rivals for two hundred thousand dollars. And John, I, I . . ."

And his partner rests him down on the bed and whispers, "That's okay. I poisoned you."

A guy is walking down the street when he sees a funeral procession going by. It's the longest funeral procession he's ever seen, with a long line of men walking behind the hearse. He notices that the first man in line has a Doberman pinscher on a leash. After watching the long line of men for a few minutes, he goes up to the first man in the procession and says, "Excuse me, sir, I'm very sorry to bother you in your time of grief, but I've never seen such a large funeral procession. Could you tell me who this funeral is for?"

And the guy, tightening the leash on the dog, says, "It's for my mother-in-law. My Doberman here attacked and killed her."

And the guy says, "I'm sorry to hear that. But tell me, do you think I could *borrow* this dog?"

And the other guy points his thumb over his shoulder and says, "Get in line."

A woman is dying and she calls her husband to her bedside.

Crying, she says, "Al, when I go, I want you to go on living. Find somebody else. Give her everything I have. My jewelry, my home, my dresses."

And her husband cries, "No, no, I can't, I can't."

And his wife says, "But you must, you simply must!"

And her husband says, "No, my darling. I really can't. You're a size fourteen and she wears an eight!"

An actor walks into the Polo Lounge of the Beverly Hills Hotel with his pet terrier, asks for a table for two. The maître d' shows them to a corner table for two. When the waiter hands the actor the menu, the actor gets upset.

"Does it look like I'm eating alone?" he says to the waiter. "Service for two!"

So the waiter brings the dog a menu and then the two of them enjoy a long, leisurely dinner.

After coffee and brandy, the waiter brings the check and places it in front of the actor.

And the actor promptly yells, "How dare you!" and throws the check in front of the dog. "Don't you understand anything? I'm his guest!"

A woman jumped into a cab outside this building, and she said, "To the maternity hospital and you don't have to rush. I just work there!"

A man and his wife go to the Poconos for a few days of rest and relaxation and sightseeing. When they check out of the hotel the clerk hands him a bill and the guy says to the clerk, "What's this twenty-five-dollar charge for?"

And the clerk says, "It's for meals." The man says, "What do you mean twenty-five dollars for meals? We ate out every meal. We didn't eat anything here at the hotel!"

And the clerk says, "It was here for you."

And the guy says, "Yeah. Well, I'm charging you twenty-five dollars for kissing my wife!"

And the clerk says, "I never kissed your wife!"

And the guy says, "Well, it was here for you!"

A bum collapses on the street and all of a sudden a large crowd gathers around him.

Some little old lady screams, "Give the poor man a drink of whiskey!"

And a bunch of people holler out, "Give him some air!"

And the little old lady says again, "Give him a drink of whiskey!"

And someone shouts out, "Call an ambulance."

The little old lady hollers out again, "Give him a drink of whiskey!"

And the crowd continues to argue back and forth.

Suddenly the old bum sits up and yells, "Will you all shut up and listen to the little old lady!"

A missionary is traveling through the jungle and he hears the sound of a native drum loud and clear.

As he comes closer he sees a witch doctor is pounding on a drum furiously. So the missionary says to the witch doctor, "Why are you beating your drum?" And the witch doctor says, "We have no water."

And the missionary says, "So, you're praying for rain?" And the witch doctor says, "No, I'm sending for the plumber."

A guy's out playing golf with a friend and he says to him, "I can only play nine holes with you today. I gotta go to my father's wedding."

And the other guy says, "Your father's wedding? You mean that old man is getting married?"

And the guy says, "Yeah, and as a matter of fact, it's going to be a short wedding 'cause *he's* got to go to *his* father's wedding."

And his friend says, "*His* father's wedding? His father must be ninety-nine years old. Why does he want to get married at ninety-nine?"

And the other guy says, "He doesn't want to. He has to!"

Neckerchief   The leader of a lynch mob.

Newport   Famous Rhode Island city, now working nights as a cigarette.

Nudist Camp Where you're seen in the best places.

Obscene The picture an *ob* paints.

Operating Room Warren Beatty's bedroom.

Operetta In Italy, a girl who works for the phone company.

Partnership What you send your wife on when you want to be alone.

Peanut Oil What you use on squeaky elephants.

A guy is working at his office and gets a terrible headache and decides he'll take the afternoon off and goes home. He gets home, goes into the kitchen, opens up the cabinet, and takes a couple of aspirin. He hears some music and walks upstairs to his bedroom and finds his wife in bed with a midget.

And he shouts at her, "I forgave you before, time and time again. And you promised only last week when I caught you, you'd never cheat on me again, and now I come home and you're in bed with a midget!"

And his wife looks up and says, "Don't be mad. Can't you see I'm trying to taper off?"

A young guy arrives in New York from the Midwest. After spending three weeks trying to meet some new friends, the guy goes to services at a church on a Sunday.

Sitting next to him is a very distinguished gentleman who starts talking to the young man. After introductions, the gentleman tells the young man that his daughter is about the same age and invites him to dinner. Well, the young guy comes over and immediately is taken with the young lady. Pretty soon it becomes a serious romance and they get married.

After they return from the honeymoon, the father calls the young man into his office and tells him he wants the young man to become partners in his business. The young man is very excited. The father-in-law says, "I'll start you off as treasurer of the company." And the young man says, "I don't know anything about math, books, and all that stuff." So the father-in-law says, "Okay, then, I'll start you off in the shipping department. You'll help get out our product, loading and billing." The young man says, "I have a bad back so I can't be lifting anything." So his father-in-law says, "I'm getting out of the business, you'll become chairman of the board." And his son-in-law says, "I don't know anything about running a business. I don't even know what we manufacture."

So his father-in-law says, "Well, what do you want me to do?"

And the kid says, "Why don't you buy me out?"

A couple check into a motel in Philadelphia opposite the railroad station. In the morning, the husband gets up early to go see some clients and leaves his wife in bed.

About an hour later, a train passes and the vibration knocks the guy's wife right out of bed. She gets up and gets back into bed and another ten minutes later another train passes and again the vibrations knock her out of bed. Fifteen minutes later the same thing happens.

So she calls up the desk clerk and tells him what she thinks of his motel. The clerk says, "I don't believe it." So she says, "Come up here and see for yourself."

So he goes to the room and she says, "I'm lying in bed and every time a train passes, the damn vibrations knock me out of bed!" And the clerk says, "I don't believe it." So the woman says, "Okay, lie down and see for yourself." He's lying in the bed five minutes when her husband walks in the door and says to the clerk, "What the hell are you doing in my bed?"

And the clerk says, "Believe it or not, I'm waiting for a train!"

The chairman of a charity fund drive undertakes a big chore by calling on a wealthy businessman and trying to get him to contribute to the charity.

The chairman gets an appointment with him and goes to his office.

And the chairman says, "You know, you've never contributed to our charity. Our survey shows you made over four hundred thousand dollars last year and we feel you should give something."

And the guy says, "Did your survey show that I have a mother with no means of support? Did it show that my sister's husband was killed in a terrible accident, leaving her with four small children? Did it show that my brother was badly injured in World War II? Well, if I don't give to them, why should I give anything to the fund?"

A Bishop in a small Midwestern town buys two parrots and teaches them to say the rosary. He even has two sets of tiny rosary beads made for them.

After months of exhaustive training, the parrots are able to recite the rosary and use the beads at the same time.

The Bishop is so pleased with the results of his endeavor that he decides to teach another parrot the rosary. So he goes to the pet store and buys a female parrot, which he brings home and puts into the cage with the other two.

As he does this and shuts the cage door, one parrot turns to the other and says, "Throw away your beads, George—our prayers have been answered!"

There's a big divorce trial going on. So the attorney for the complainant in the case puts his client on the stand.

And the attorney, very sympathetically, says to his client on the stand, "Now, as I understand it, every night when you came home from work you'd find a different man hiding in the closet."

And the man says, "Yes, that's right."

And his lawyer says, "Of course, all this caused you untold anguish, heartaches, and suffering. Right?"

And the guy says, "It sure did! I never had any place to hang up my coat!"

There's this book salesman who's just terrible looking. He's pale, sickly, and really seedy looking. And he tries to see the head of this bookstore chain and every time he comes in to try and get an appointment with him, they say, "No."

Well, one day the book salesman manages to trap the bookstore chain owner as he gets on the elevator and says, "This book is perfect for your stores. Please—take an order from me. You'll thank me for it later!"

So the owner says, "What's the name of it?"

And the salesman says, "*Health, Wealth, and Happiness.*"

So the owner gives the salesman a quick glance and says, "Okay, I'll buy it, on the condition that *you* read it!"

And the salesman says, "Read it—I wrote it!"

There's a traveling salesman going through the mountains of Kentucky and he stops at a hillbilly's home and gets into a conversation with a character named Zeke. And he says to the hillbilly, "Zeke, is that your boy milking the cows?" and the hillbilly says, "Yes, sir, that's my son Lem."

And the salesman says, "Lem's quite a big boy. How old is he?" And the hillbilly says, "He's about fourteen years old, I guess." And the salesman says, "What's he going to do—stay around these hills?"

And the hillbilly says, "Yes, sir, just like we all did."

And the salesman says, "Why don't you send Lem to the big city and give him an education, so when he grows up, he'll learn something?" The salesman says, "I have a friend who has a little store in New York City—up in the Bronx. He'll give Lem a job, then he can go to night school and learn something." So the hillbilly says, "I guess you're right. Maybe he should get a little education."

So arrangements are made and Lem goes to New York.

But all the neighbors tell Lem's folks that the big city is gonna change him and he won't be a hillbilly any more. So the hillbilly begins to worry. Three years go by and Lem comes back home on the train—and when the train pulls in and Lem gets off, his father Zeke is there to meet him, and he says, "Lem, tell me the truth, did you change?"

And Lem looks at his father and says, "No, Papa—vonce a hillbilly—alvays a hillbilly!"

A nervous young man goes to a psychiatrist for the first time and explains to the doctor that his family insisted on the visit.

The young guy tells the psychiatrist that his family is upset and demanded he seek help because he preferred cotton socks to woolen ones.

The psychiatrist says, "I think this whole thing is absurd. There's no reason for you to see me. In fact, I myself prefer cotton socks."

And the young man breaks into a smile and says, "Really? Do you like yours with oil and vinegar or just a squeeze of lemon?"

A guy comes into a bar with a small white mouse in his pocket. He puts the mouse on the bar and orders a martini for himself and a thimbleful for the mouse.

After downing the drink, the mouse stands up on its hind legs and sings a medley of songs from *My Fair Lady* ("I have often walked down this street before," "Get me to the church on time," "The rain in Spain falls mainly on the plain").

The bartender is amazed. He's in shock.

So the guy says, "Listen, buy us a round of drinks and you can keep the mouse."

So the bartender serves the drinks and says, "I can't believe that you're giving away a gold mine like that for just a few drinks."

And the guy says, "Hell, all he knows is *My Fair Lady!*"

A man dreams that he dies and goes to heaven. At six o'clock in the morning, they put him to work shining the pearly gates, the stars, cleaning up heaven, right and left. He has to work till six o'clock at night. After several days of this, he can't stand it any longer and asks if he can take a rest. So they give him two days off. So he decides he'll visit hell and see what it's like down there.

So he arrives in hell at nine o'clock in the morning and everybody is just sitting around doing nothing.

So the guy goes up to an attendant and says, "I don't get it, I'm up in heaven and what happens to me? They work my buns off from six in the morning till six at night every day. And down here where things are supposed to be tougher, you're all sitting around at nine o'clock in the morning doing nothing!"

So the attendant says, "Well, that's easy to explain. You see, there are more of us down here, so we get finished sooner."

A guy goes to a psychiatrist for six months. Suddenly one day the psychiatrist says to him, "You've got to give up smoking, you've just got to give up smoking."

And the patient looks up at him and says, "Give up smoking? That'll help me?" And the doctor says, "No—but you'll stop burning holes in my couch!"

There's this jealous husband who is sure his wife has a boyfriend. So he hires a detective to shadow her and take movies of what he sees. A few weeks later the detective reports back to the husband and tells him he has some film of his wife running around on him. "Here it is, all the evidence, and with your best friend, too!"

So they run the film and the husband sees pictures of his wife and his best friend as they have lunch, go swimming, bowling, dancing, walking and laughing in the park. After the film is over, the husband just sits there, shaking his head, and says, "I just can't believe it, I just can't believe it!"

And the detective says, "You better believe it, the evidence is all here!"

And the husband says, "That's not what I mean. I just can't believe that my wife could be so much fun!"

A guy from the Midwest comes to New York for the first time. And all day and into the night he hits all the bars in Times Square and after being in the last one, he walks out and falls down a stairway leading to the subway.

About a half-hour later, he stumbles up the stairway and runs into a pal who has been looking for him.

And his friend says, "Where in the world have you been?"

And the drunk, still glassy-eyed, says, "Down in some guy's cellar, and boy, has he got a set of trains!"

There's this guy who belonged to an organization with a lot of social benefits and each person in the club was asked to buy a cemetery plot at a reduced rate—sort of a group plan so that they'd have a place to live when they died.

But when the club finds out that the plan wasn't paying off too well, they asked the president to talk to the delinquent members and Jones was the first to be called.

So the president says to him, "You bought a plot twenty-five years ago and you haven't paid for it yet."

And Mr. Jones says, "I didn't use it!" And the president says to him, "Who stopped you?"

A successful businessman from Scarsdale goes to Cleveland on a business trip. He registers at a hotel, goes to his room, and find two blondes in his bed.

So he says, "I hate to disappoint you, girls, but I happen to be a highly respected member of my community. I'm married, the father of three children, and president of the Chamber of Commerce. I couldn't afford to have my name linked with any scandal. I'm sorry—but one of you will have to leave!"

A Frenchman comes to America and spends some time and then he returns home and he tells all his friends about all the wonders of our nation and the hospitality of the American people.

He tells his friends, "Those Americans are the most generous people I have ever seen. You eat in the best restaurants—free! You ride around in high-powered sports cars and chauffeured limousines—free! You get beautiful jewelry—free! You get all the latest clothes—free! You live in a beautiful penthouse—free! I tell you, it's marvelous."

And his friend says to him, "You mean all this happened to you?"

And the guy says, "Oh, no, not to me—to my sister!"

An ad appears in the paper one morning asking for an individual who can type, take dictation, program a computer, and speak more than one language.

The first applicant for the job is a dog. The dog is able to type 145 words per minute, takes perfect dictation, and not only can program a computer but has written several programming manuals.

The prospective boss has the dog demonstrate all these skills and then turns to him and says, "I'm really amazed by your qualifications. So I only have one final question: What about the language requirement?"

And the dog looks at him and says, "Meow!"

A mother in the Bronx walks into her son's room and says, "Hey, get up, sonny boy, you're late for school!"

And her son says, "I'm not going to school!"

"Why not?" his mother says.

And he says, "Well, for two reasons. All the kids hate me and all the teachers hate me."

And his mother says, "Well, I'll give you two reasons why you should go to school."

And her son says, "Yeah? Name them!"

And his mother says, "One, you're forty-five years old, and two, you're the principal!"

A lawyer is in court defending a client who is accused of bigamy. And the fight goes on for weeks. It's in all the papers. He's accused of being married to more than one woman and as the trial ends, the wealthy businessman is acquitted.

So the lawyer embraces him after the verdict and says to him, "Hey, you're a free man. Go on home to your wife!"

And the guy says to his lawyer, "Which one?"

A ninety-five-year-old man is sitting on a park bench crying and sobbing. A friendly policeman stops and asks him, "Are you feeling all right?" And the elderly gentleman says, "Yes. I'm feeling all right." The policeman says, "Did your wife pass away?" And the old man says, "No." The policeman then asks him if his wife has left him? And the old gentleman says, "No. I'm ninety-five years old and my wife is twenty-six." And the policeman asks him if he's having any problems sexually and the man says, "No, not at all. We have relations three or four times a week." And the policeman asks him, "Is your wife a terrible cook?" And again the man says, "No. She's a marvelous cook. She's studied at the finest gourmet schools in France." "Then you must be hard up for cash?" the cop asks. And the old man says, "No. I'm very well off and my wife is wealthy." The cop says, "Then why are you crying if everything is as great as you say they are?" And the old man looks up and says, "I'm lost!"

A mother takes her little boy to a psychiatrist and asks him, "Can a ten-year-old boy marry a beautiful star like Elizabeth Taylor?"

And the psychiatrist says, "Of course not, it's impossible."

And the mother looks down at the kid and says, "See, what did I tell you. Now go and get a divorce!"

A seventh-grader comes home late from his suburban school and his mother is frantic. And she asks him, "What happened to you?"

And the young boy replies, "Well, I was made traffic guard today, Mama, and all the kids have to wait for my signal, after I stop a car, before they can cross the street!"

And his mother says, "But you were due home *two hours ago!*"

And the kid looks up to her and says, "Mama, do you know how long I had to wait before a car came along I could stop!?"

A guy leaves his office early one day and when he gets home he discovers his beautiful wife in bed with a neighbor. So the guy says, "Well, since you're sleeping with my wife, I'm going over and sleep with yours."

And his neighbor says, "Go ahead. You probably need the rest!"

Prude   A prune with no manners.

Richard the Lion-Hearted   Survivor of world's first transplant.

There's an old bum living on the streets in New York. One day he hears that his brother is very sick in Los Angeles.

So by working day and night on the street, he's able to beg enough money to buy his airline ticket. He goes to JFK Airport, stumbles up to the ticket counter, and plunks down all his money. The clerk counts the money and says to the bum, "I'm sorry, sir, but you're a nickel short."

So the bum tells the clerk he'll be right back. He runs out in front of the terminal, stops the first man he sees, and says to the guy, "Mister, can you let me have a nickel so I can get to California?"

The guy looks at the seedy bum, hands him a quarter, and says, "Here. Take four of your friends!"

A missionary gets lost in the jungle and while he's wandering around looking for members of his group he's confronted by a huge lion that starts to chase him through the jungle. After running for a short while, the lion corners the missionary and, with no other option, the missionary drops to his knee and starts to pray. And as he looks up in a suddenly quiet moment, to his surprise he sees the lion is also praying. So the missionary says to the lion, "This is miraculous, joining me in prayer when I had given myself up for lost."

And the lion looks up and says to him, "Don't interrupt. I'm saying grace!"

There's a guy who goes into the Claridge Hotel in Atlantic City every night and begs the guests for money. He goes up to anyone in the casino and says, "Just loan me a hundred dollars. I'll double it in no time and pay you right back."

But night after night everybody just shakes their head no and walks away.

One night the guy runs into a generous oil man from Texas who hands him a crisp one-hundred-dollar bill and says, "Here, boy, enjoy yourself!"

The guy thanks the Texan and walks over to the blackjack table and blows the whole hundred in five minutes.

The next night he sees the Texan again and again asks him for some money. Again the Texan gives him another one-hundred-dollar bill and again, in a matter of minutes, the money is gone.

This goes on for three weeks. Every night the Texan gives him money and every night the money is gone almost as soon the guy gets it.

Finally, in desperation and frustration, the unhappy guy tells one of his friends about his experience with the generous Texan. And the guy's friend says to him, "There's only one thing to do. Lose the bum. He's bad luck for you!"

There are two psychiatrists who have offices on the same floor in a building. At the end of a hot day, the two get in the elevator together. The younger doctor, about forty, says to his elderly colleague, who's in his seventies, "I don't know how you do it. I'm completely done in and you're older and you look fresh as a spring morning. How can you look so great after listening to babbling patients from morning till night?"

And the older psychiatrist says, "Who listens?"

There is this doctor who goes up to his friend, who also happens to be a doctor. So he says to his friend, "I understand you've been having a romance with my wife and I'd like to know what you think about her lovemaking?"

And the other doctor says, "You're married to her and you want to know what I think? Why?"

And the other doctor says, "Why? I'd like a second opinion!"

A businessman is sitting quietly in a restaurant eating lunch when suddenly a stranger comes over to his table and says, "Hey there, Fellman. My goodness, what happened to you? You used to be short, now you're tall. You used to be blond, now you're dark-haired. You used to have blue eyes, now they're brown!"

And the businessman looks up at the guy and says, "I beg your pardon, sir, but my name's not Fellman."

And the guy says, "My gosh! You changed your name, too!"

A flying saucer lands in Central Park and a crowd gathers to witness the phenomenon.

As the smoke and exhaust clear from the landed craft, a door on the space ship opens and a green man with six arms appears. After the screams of bewilderment die out, a man from the crowd approaches the man from outer space and he asks, "Are you from Mars?" And the green man replies, "Yes." And the spectator asks, "Do you all have antennas sticking out of your head?" And again the martian answers, "Yes." And then the man asks him, "Do you all have little black caps on top of your head?"

And the martian says, "Only the orthodox!"

There's an elderly man who is going to celebrate his hundredth birthday and a reporter of a local paper calls on him for an interview.

After the reporter congratulates the man, he asks him, "To what do you attribute your longevity?" And the old man pauses for a moment and then holding up his hand and counting off the items on his fingers, he says, "I never smoked, drank alcohol, or overate, and I always get up every morning at six."

So the reporter says, "But I had an uncle who did the exact same things you did and yet he only lived to be eighty. How do you account for that?"

And the old man looks at him and says, "He didn't keep it up long enough!"

A guy is working late at the office and he invites his pretty secretary out to dinner. Then they go dancing and then back to her apartment and they make love.

Later on, when the guy is ready to leave, he asks her for a piece of chalk, which he puts behind his ear, and then he goes home.

When he gets home his wife asks him what kept him so long and the guy tells her the truth: "We worked late, so I took my secretary out to dinner and then we went back to her place and made love!"

And his wife hollers, "Liar! I know you were playing pool. You've still got the chalk behind your ear!"

A reporter from a newspaper goes up to three senior citizens sitting on a park bench in St. Petersburg and he asks the first one, "What do you all do all day?" And the old man says, "Nothing." Then he asks the second senior citizen, "And what do you do all day?" And the old gentleman also replies, "Nothing."

Finally he asks the third senior citizen, "What do you do all day?" And the old gentleman says, "Are you kidding? What do I do all day? In this glorious land of sunshine, contentment, natural beauty, clean air, and unlimited opportunity—what do I do all day? Is that what you're asking?"

And the reporter says, "Yes."

And the old man says, "I help them!"

There's a tourist standing in line at the train station and he sees another guy carrying two heavy suitcases—grunting, straining, sweating! He also sees that the man is wearing headphones.

The guy wearing headphones is snapping his fingers, sort of moving around on his feet. "Hey, man," the guy says. "Wanna listen to some great stereo music?" So he hands the headphones to the tourist who is immediately impressed with the quality of sound coming from the small radio and headphones. So the tourist says, "Wow, that's really remarkable to get that good sound and that much volume from such a small radio. I'd like to buy it." So the tourist buys the radio and headphones and as he starts to walk away, the other guy, pointing to the suitcases, says, "Wanna buy the batteries, too?"

Roasted Peanuts Peanuts that are honored by their friends who tell risque jokes about them.

Robin Redbreast Bird who wears a tight bra.

Salem Lights Bulbs you put on a boat when you go out in the water.

Sex What follows five.

Sex Symbol What a drummer plays with to get turned on.

Sleep That which when you don't get enough of, you wake up half a . . .

A young guy just out of college writes his parents that he's engaged to a wonderful girl and he's bringing her home for the holidays so they can meet her. He tells them that she's the girl of his dreams, that she's lovely, beautiful, and has a great sense of humor. So the parents get the house ready and in a few days their son arrives with his fiancée.

They no sooner come into the house and they all hug and kiss. Then the father calls his son aside and whispers, "You said she was young; she's almost forty. You said she was gorgeous; she looks like a plucked chicken. Look at her legs: she's bowlegged and looks like death warmed over. You said . . ." And the son says, "You don't have to whisper. She's hard of hearing, too!"

There's a big temperance lecture going on and the preacher screams out his warning about the evils of John Barleycorn.

"Who's the richest man in town?" he shouts. "The saloon keeper! Who has the biggest home? The saloon keeper! Who has the finest clothes? The saloon keeper! And who pays for all this? You do, my friends. You do!"

A few days later an old drunk who had been in the audience stops the preacher on the street and congratulates him on his rousing speech.

So the preacher says, "I'm glad to see you've given up drinking."

And the bum says, "Well, not exactly. I've bought a saloon!"

Two guys are having a drink at a bar and one of the guys says to his pal, "Hey, did you hear the one about the two Jews that got off a bus and one says to the other—"

And his pal says, "Wait a minute, what's wrong with you? Why must it always be two Jews? Two Jews—always we tell stories to abuse the Jews. They have enough trouble. Why don't you pick on some other nationality for a change?"

And his friend says, "Okay, if that's how you feel about it. Two Chinamen get off a bus and one says to the other, 'Are you coming to my son's Bar Mitzvah?'. . ."

A drunk walks into a candy shop. And a lady clerk waits on him and says, "May I help you, sir?"

And the lush says, "Do you have them candies with liquor in the middle?"

And the clerk says, "Yes, sir, we do."

And the drunk says, "Okay, gimme a fifth of middles!"

A man enters a psychiatrist's office, sits down in a chair, takes a tobacco pouch from his pocket, and begins stuffing pipe tobacco into his left ear.

The psychiatrist says, "Well, Mr. Abernathy, you've certainly come to the right place. Can I help you?"

And the man looks up and says, "Yeah. Have you got a light?"

Two girls go out for a night on the town. After a couple of drinks they go to a disco. They're no sooner at their table when a rather nice-looking guy comes over and asks one of them to dance.

As they embrace and start to dance, the young girl says to the guy, "You're very pale looking. You look like you've never been out in the sun." And the guy says, "That's because I just got out of prison." And the girl retorts, "Prison? What were you in for?" And the guy replies, "I stabbed my wife to death, cut off her head, and threw her body in the river." And the girl looks over to her friend at the table and yells, "Barbara, he's single!"

One day three turtles go on a picnic down by the river. They've got the picnic basket filled with all kinds of sandwiches. Just as they arrive down by the river it starts to rain, so they decide that one of them must go back after an umbrella so they won't get wet while they eat.

The smallest turtle agrees to go if the other two promise they won't eat the sandwiches while he's gone. They all agree to the terms and the little turtle leaves.

Now, they wait a day, a week, a month, until finally a year goes by. Still the turtle does not return. So finally one of the turtles says to the other, "He's not coming back. Let's go ahead and eat the sandwiches."

Just then the little turtle sticks his head from behind a nearby rock and says, "If you do, I won't go!"

An eighty-year-old man marries a twenty-year-old girl and a friend of his advises him, "Take in a boarder if you want to be happy and keep your twenty-year-old bride happy." So the old man says, "That's a great idea," and he decides to try it.

A few months later the old man runs into his friend and his friend asks, "How's the young bride?"

And the old man says happily, "Okay. She's pregnant, you know." And his friend says, "Hey, it looks like my plan worked. And how is that boarder of yours?"

And the old man says, "Fine, fine. She's pregnant, too!"

A big-game hunter is in the deepest jungles of Africa. One day he gets separated from the rest of the safari and he finds himself lost. Weeks go by and he's still missing. During this time the guy has built a little shelter and he is doing all he can to stay alive.

They send a search party, which after a few weeks finds the little shelter just as the guy is ready to collapse from hunger and fever.

So the rescue party knocks on the door. And the guy asks weakly, "Who is it?" And one of the rescuers says, "The Red Cross." And the dying man says, "I gave at the office."

Late one night a doctor gets an excited call from a woman.

And the woman says, "Doctor, you've got to come over right away. I think my husband's dead in bed!"

The doctor, who knows the guy is a big drinker, says, "Stick him with a pin and let me know if he moves." And the woman says, "Okay."

A half hour later she calls back to the doctor and she's crying, "Doctor, can you meet me at the hospital?"

And the doctor says, "Weren't you able to rouse your husband?"

And the woman says, "Oh, the pin worked all right. But he hit me in the mouth and I'm gonna need stitches!"

A guy is walking down the street and he's moaning because of the pain he's got from a terrible toothache. He meets a friend of his on the street, and the friend asks how he is and the guy says, "How am I? I've got the worst toothache I've ever had in my life. What should I do? Do you have any suggestions?"

And the other guy says, "You know, when I have a toothache or a pain, I go to my wife, and she puts her arms around me and kisses and caresses me and comforts me till I forget all about the pain. You ought to try that."

And the other guy, holding his jaw, says, "Gee, that's wonderful—is she home now?"

A beautiful zebra arrives at the Bronx Zoo and an African pony tells a buddy of his about the zebra's sexual appetite. So the pony wastes no time and saunters over to the zebra.

An hour later the pony returns to his quarters and his skin is torn up and he's bleeding, one ear is hanging down to his knee, his tail is half torn off, and his friend says, "Well, was she everything I said?" And the beat-up pony says, "I don't know, I couldn't even get off the pajamas!"

A reporter goes to see one of the big generals at Cape Kennedy to find out how accurate our missiles are. So after he's asked, the general says, "From Cape Kennedy we can hit targets in Miami, Fort Lauderdale, and Tampa."

So the reporter says, "How about Soviet targets? Can you hit Russian targets?"

And the general says, "Yeah, if they're located in Miami, Ft. Lauderdale, or Tampa!"

Two guys are sitting at a bar having a drink. And one of them says to the other, "Do you like fat, sloppy women who roll their stockings down below their knees?" And the other guy says, "Yuch! I should say not." And the guy says, "Well, let me ask you this, do you like women who always smell from garlic and have false teeth?"

And the other guy says, "Sounds horrible—of course not!" And the other guy says, "So, why are you always trying to date my wife?"

A guy accidentally swallows a Ping-Pong ball. Well, not exactly accidentally. Stupidly is more the word. See, he beats this guy in Ping-Pong and when he jumps over the net to shake his hand, he breaks the table in two and jabs his paddle in his nose and swallows a Ping-Pong ball.

So they rush him to surgery to have it removed. But the guy says to the doctor he wants a local anesthetic so he can watch the operation.

So he winces a little as the first incision is made, even though he doesn't feel it. And he doesn't feel the next cut, or the next. After a couple of minutes more of incisions, and the doctor is cutting here, he's cutting there, in a rather random manner, and the guy says to the doctor, "Why do you have to cut in so many places? They don't seem to be consistent." And the doctor, who is cutting away, says, "That's the way the ball bounces!"

A young man working at an office goes in to see his boss and asks him if he could have the rest of the day off.

And the boss asks him, "What for?" And the guy says, "My wife's gonna have a baby."

So the understanding employer gives him the rest of the day off. When the young clerk comes to work the following morning the boss calls him into the office and says, "Congratulations! Was it a boy or a girl?"

And the clerk says, "Oh, it's much too soon to tell. We have to wait nine months to find that out."

Two drunks are staggering down a railroad track and after walking over a mile one of them turns to the other and says, "Man, I'm tired. I sure wish we'd get to the bottom of these stairs."

And the other drunk looks up and says, "These stairs aren't so bad, but these low bannisters are killing me!"

A woman goes into the Missing Persons Bureau and claims to the officer in charge that her husband has disappeared.

So the sergeant starts to fill out the necessary papers. He asks the lady if she can give him a description of the missing man.

"Certainly," says the woman. "He was twenty-nine years old, six feet three inches tall, blond hair, handsome, well dressed, and speaks flawless English."

A friend of hers is standing alongside and pulls the woman aside and says, "Martha, what are you talking about? Your husband is bald, fat, and forty."

And the woman looks at her and says, "I know, I know. But who wants *him* back?"

> **Solvent** The answer to the question: "Vere is Sol?"
>
> **Stalemates** Elizabeth Taylor's five ex-husbands.
>
> **Stopwatch** The command a policeman gives to a Rolex who's going too fast.

A young husband just married a couple of weeks comes home from a really hard day at the office. And as soon as he comes in, he falls down on the couch, worn out, frazzled and froozled.

And his bride comes in and looks at him very sympathetically and says, "Darling, you look so tired and hungry. How would you like a nice steak smothered with onions, a green vegetable, some french fried potatoes, and some delicious pie à la mode?"

And the weary new bridegroom looks up and says, "Not tonight, honey, I'm too tired to go out!"

A little boy in second grade says to his teacher, "I ain't got no pencil."

And the teacher says, "It's I *don't* have a pencil.—*I* don't have a pencil; *you* don't have a pencil;—*we* don't have any pencils;—*they* don't have any pencils. Is that clear?"

And the kid says, "No. What happened to all them pencils?"

It's a beautiful day in the park and a young father is pushing a baby carriage in which a baby is screaming his head off. And as the father wheels the baby along, he keeps murmuring, "Easy now, Donald. Just keep calm, Donald, steady boy. It's all right, Donald. Just relax, Donald. It's gonna be all right, Donald . . ."

And a mother passes by and says to the guy pushing the carriage, "You certainly know how to talk to an upset child—quietly and gently." And she leans over the carriage and says, "What seems to be the trouble, Donald?"

And the father says, "Oh, no. *He's* Henry. *I'm* Donald."

It's a beautiful sunny afternoon and there are two nuns sitting in Shea Stadium watching the Mets.

Sitting in back of them are a couple of guys drinking beer. One of the guys says to his friend, "You can't see a thing, these nuns' hats are blocking the whole game. Remind me to move to Cleveland where only 10 percent of the people are Catholics."

And his drinking buddy says, "Hey, let's go to Omaha, where only 5 percent are Catholic."

One of the nuns turns around and says, "I got a better idea. Why don't both of you go to hell where you won't find *any* Catholics?"

Supertramp   High-priced New York call girl.

Trash Bags   Groupies that hang around garbage
    men.

It's a typical pub in Dublin, and a guy walks in
and over to the bar. His face is black and blue and
beaten to a pulp. So the bartender says to him, "Who
did that to you?"

And the guy says, "I had a fight with Mike Shan-
non!"

And the bartender takes a deep gulp and says to
him, "What? You let a little guy like that beat you
up? You ought to be ashamed of yourself, a little
good-for-nothing runt like that Mike!"

And the guy says, "Hold on there. Don't be talking disrespectfully of the dead!"

Late one evening at a convention in Atlantic City,
four happy delegates come stumbling drunk out of a
hotel and the doorman puts them in a taxi and tells
the driver, "This one goes to the Tropicana, these
two go to the Claridge and the one with the hiccups
goes to the Sands." And the car leaves.

In a few minutes the taxi is back with everybody
still in it.

And the driver whistles to the doorman, who
comes over, and the driver says to him, "Would you
mind sorting these fellows out again? I hit a bump!"

A guy is at a bar after office hours and he says to his friend, "Boy, I just have to have another drink before I go home. My wife is on my back from the moment I get home till I leave the next day about money. She's always nagging me about money. Last week she wanted two hundred dollars. The day before yesterday, it was one hundred. And this morning she asked for another one hundred and fifty dollars."

And his friend says, "Wow, that's awful. What could she possibly do with all that money?"

And the guy says, "I don't know. I never give her any!"

Three guys arrive at the pearly gates. So St. Peter looks at the first one and says, "Where are you from?" And the guy answers, "Chicago!" And St. Peter says, "You can go to hell!" Then he turns to the second man and asks him where he came from and the guy says, "Los Angeles!" And again St. Peter says, "And you can go to hell!"

The third guy doesn't even wait for the question. He says, "St. Peter, I'm from Texas. Do I go to hell, too?"

And St. Peter shakes his head sadly, motions him through the gate, and says, "No, son—you've already been there!"

There's a dirty, seedy-looking bum lounging in front of the New York Athletic Club one day when one of the club officials comes out and asks him to move along.

When the bum refuses to move, the official grabs him and throws him into the street. So the bum picks himself up from the curb and says to the guy, "Who do you think you are throwing me into the street?"

And the man says, "I am the secretary of the club."

And the bum looks up and says, "Well, this is a hell of a way to get new members!"

Two guys plan to go hunting and they're all excited about it.

One guy says, "I'll bring all the hunting paraphernalia and you bring the provisions."

The morning they're ready to leave, the guy who's responsible for the provisions shows up with a loaf of bread and four bottles of whiskey.

So the other guy says, "I don't believe you. I leave it to you and what happens? You bring a loaf of bread and four bottles of whiskey. Now, what the hell are we going to do with all that bread?"

Virus   What people who can't spell pneumonia get.

Walnuts   People who are crazy about walls.

Wax Museum   How you would describe Howard Cosell's ears.

A Bishop and a Congressman go to heaven, arrive at the pearly gates and St. Peter greets them and says that he's going to give them immediate room assignments.

So St. Peter hands the Bishop some keys and says, "Here you are, the keys to one of our nicest efficiency units. And, for you, Mr. Congressman, the keys to our finest penthouse suite."

And the Bishop says, "Wait a minute. This is unfair."

And St. Peter says, "Listen, Bishops are a dime a dozen up here, but this is the first Congressman we've ever seen!"

A woman expecting her seventh child decides that the time has come to tell her children about the blessed event. So she calls everybody into the living room and she says, "The stork will be coming to pay us a visit!"

And her husband looks up from his newspaper and says, "A visit! What do you mean visit? He lives here!"

A father says to his daughter, "Your boyfriend Harold talked to me last night and asked for your hand in marriage and I want you to know that I consented."

And the girl hugs her father and starts crying and says, "I don't want to leave my mother."

And the father looks into his daughter's teary eyes and says, "I understand, my dear. Only don't let me stand in the way of your happiness. Take your mother with you!"

Worship   A boat WURS ride in.

A census taker in Philadelphia was questioning a woman with six kids aged two months to seven years and he said to her, "Maybe I misunderstood you. Did you say your husband died four years ago?" She said, "That's right." And he just looked at the kids—especially the baby—so the woman says, "He died—I didn't!"

Two goats are busy eating garbage. While they're eating, one of them finds a roll of old film and proceeds to eat it up. After he finishes chewing up the film, the other goat asks him, "Did you enjoy the film?" And the other goat says, "Actually, I preferred the book!"

A beer salesman from St. Louis goes to Cardinal O'Connor and says to him, "Your Eminence, I'm from the Budweiser Company, and if you would change the prayer from 'give us this day our daily bread' to 'give us this day our daily brew,' we'd be willing to contribute a million dollars to your church." And the Cardinal tells him in no uncertain terms that he should be ashamed of himself and asks him to leave.

Later that day at a bar, the young salesman tells his troubles to the bartender. The bartender tells the salesman, "The Cardinal doesn't make the rules. You have to talk to the Pope."

So the guy goes to Italy and gets an audience with the Pope. He approaches the Pope and says, "Your Holiness, I represent the Budweiser Company in St. Louis, and if you would change the prayer from 'give us this day our daily bread' to 'give us this day our daily brew,' we'd donate a million dollars to the church."

So the Pope thinks for a moment, turns to his secretary, and says, "Bishop, when does our contract with Wonderbread expire?"